Explaining the circumstances

Christopher North

Oversteps Books

First published in 2010 by   Oversteps Books Ltd
                                  6 Halwell House
                                  South Pool
                                  Nr Kingsbridge
                                  Devon
                                  TQ7 2RX
                                  UK

www.overstepsbooks.com

Oversteps Books acknowledges with thanks the financial
assistance of Arts Council England, South West

Printed in Great Britain by imprint digital, Devon.

for Marisa

and in memory of my father Arthur North, 1921–2009

Acknowledgements:
prizes and publications

Thanks are due to the editors of the following magazines
in which some of these poems appeared: North, Wolf,
Smiths Knoll, Brittle Star, Cadenza, Acumen, South Bank,
Interpreter's House, Templar anthology and Cimarron Review.

Battlefield was included in the Faber Book of Landscape Poetry.
Taino was Highly Commended in the Forward nominations
for best single poem of 2009. First prizes were won by:
Sorting old Kodachromes (Speakeasy), *Mike's Word for the
Day* (Segora), *The Wind on the Day Simon Left* (Writer's
Forum), *Geese in a Market Crowd* (Plough Short Poems),
Ascension of Isla Guilio (Newark), *They Were Just Going to
Work* (Newark), and *Thessalonians* (East Yorks).

The photograph on the back cover is by Bernard Battley;
and the cover illustration was photographed in Seville by
Christopher North.

Contents

The Company of the Invisible

The architect,
who designed a rejected baluster rail for the Oxo building,
had a drink with Kirsty on the same day a scream she'd made
tripping on some steps delivering software to a recording
studio had been dubbed into a sequence in a Madonna video
they were doing. They used it for a moment when the diva
leapt from a car but it wasn't acknowledged in the credits
– that sort of video doesn't have credits they said.

He also mentioned
a tall and hearty man he'd met at a rodeo in Salinas,
California, who had a short-term contract with
Warner Brothers to guffaw in the soundtrack of a cartoon
series they were making about a family of donkeys;
but his guffaw wasn't used. One of the in-house cartoonists
found he could copy it. So the hearty man remained a janitor
but would always produce the guffaw if asked at parties.
He maintained a positive attitude and opined that, after all,
they got to the guffaw they needed by way of his –
he'd been a link in the chain. He'd played a part and wasn't
bitter – just another day at the wrong end of the telescope.

And then
there was that ornate conservatory extension with structural
trouble on the back of a house in Amersham that I'd saved
by some sound advice during my surveying days.
Every morning I would drive past and mutely salute
my contribution to that corner of Metro-land
until, that is, last week when the whole thing was demolished
to make way for a block of flats.

Mike's Word for the Day

The first one I remember was 'stipendiary' –
in flooded roast beef, the puddings of Pudding Lane,
hurled pies and for some reason
the rhythm of a bicycle pump filling a tyre.

The next day 'pip' led to *For God's sake get a grip Pippa!*
shouted across a cold morning lake – a brown lake
with various dark, litter filled side ponds
and a terrier yapping frantically on the bank.

Then came 'moist' delivered after considerable hesitation.
Uncertainty was unusual. On Monday he was absent:
a vacant chair, drawers emptied, desk top cleared –
all we were left with was Friday's 'moist'.

As the week crawled on we tried 'crumpling',
'crutch' and, the last I remember, 'vulpine'
but the magic was gone. Another took his chair.
Sucked boiled sweets. Spoke with a lisp.

Gull

Returning from the hospital, a blustery day,
a glimpse of sea with flecks of white on lead –
clouds uneasy, hard edge cumulus on the horizon.

Suddenly, crossing the road in front of us,
a gull. Expressionless, self-involved,
it was hurrying, slightly late for an appointment.

Near the verge it broke into a little run
and we could see it carried a broken wing,
seemingly clutching to its side – a brief-case.

The wing was held by a tendon only.
The gull settled by a thistle and faced the road
to wait routinely for the morning bus.

The Wind on the Day Simon Left

Outside his office evening wind filled the cedars.
An obvious association involved galleons
side by side on the froth of a marble sea
but this was surface only

although it's true I felt currents
that jaunted and raced about headlands,
drenched over rocks, slammed doors
and threw sudden spray on bleary window glass.

We talked calmly; anxious to maintain straight partings,
neat ties, shaken hands, all the required facades;
but delivering final boxes to the car we became wild men,
the wind making our hair suddenly neanderthal,

in our nostrils the smell of forest.

Eurostar

Nikki, Nikki I need your help desperately.
He's arriving at Amsterdam barefoot at eleven see,
and I don't mind him bare foot for a couple of days,
in fact it'll do him good but I want to ride him Friday
so he'll need shoes by then. Can you fix it for me?

Billy, look, we're in a head hunt situation here.
If he's spooked about the travel, I know it's tough
but tell him no. We just want cream, no fuss.
If we stick to those criteria we set out over lunch,
(in Berlin wasn't it?), nothing can stop us.

Hey Ben, can we have a quiet drink sometime?
You're breaking up Ben. Pesky tunnels! No, that's better.
Look I can't keep up with this thing.
I'm so tired. I don't want to sound a quitter
but ... Ben can you hear? Can you hear me?

Nikki, how do I know what a farrier is in French?
Has anybody phoned? Oh I love him so and I miss him.
I just need to know that he landed safe and everything.
I'm going into the tunnel for twenty minutes,
when I'm on the other side gimme a ring.

Billy, listen to me, I've got quality heads, loads of them.
I can slice off the dimbos and dumbos and backfill.
I can do that. What do you think? Maybe you me do
an hour on Tuesday, no Wednesday, at Frankfurt
and flesh it out; get the numbers crunched through.

I'm so tired Ben. Haven't slept right for a week.
Another month like this I'll fall out the net.
I'm just too wired up. Must go! Someone wants me.
Hey Nikki, has any one talked to my horsey yet?
How is my darling horsey?

Bovingdon Hertfordshire - 1953

A humiliation blocked out the place till now –
    some pale boy from the village prefabs.

On my way home from school
    he would wait behind a tree,

tattered raincoat, large yellow teeth,
    face pinched mean before little acts of violence.

Nearby had been an aerodrome
    but all you could see was empty flatness.

There was still a crashed bomber
    up against the fence – white star

on a blue ground and a shrapnel hole
    I worshipped in the one intact wing.

No planes came,
    though I was always looking for them.

There was a place to retreat to
    beneath the dining table with barley sugar legs

where I thumbed 'I-Spy Aircraft' to disintegration.
    There was a tree outside my bedroom window,

I watched for winking lights beyond it –
    Lancasters returning from a mission

or Dakotas: wings flicked up when approaching,
    swept back when overhead,

pert Spitfires, roaring Hurricanes
    and the Vulcan, the Comet, the Meteor.

Explaining the Circumstances

Some of these lines quote statements made on actual motor accident insurance claim forms.

Coming home I drove into the wrong house
and collided with a tree I don't have.
I crossed a garden that receded and receded
and met some people who chose to remain silent.
Time braked and the clock hands fell to six;
a drop from the tap hovered an inch above the bowl.
I saw a slow-moving, sad faced old gentleman
as he bounced off the roof of my car.

Then an invisible car came out of nowhere,
struck my car and vanished.
The road became a fan of streaked permanganate
as my left hand took flight in a cloud of feathers.
These events ceased with a clatter of Chinese thunder
as coloured rain showered through the greenhouse roof.
I stared and stared at the rising waters
and a pedestrian hit me and went under my car.

Later in an attempt to kill a fly,
I ran into a telegraph pole.
The hay field rolled over and went to sleep,
spores of bracket fungus seethed from the old oak
and a rain-coated female person said repeatedly:
'You must stop this! You must stop this!'
I had been driving for forty years
when I fell asleep at the wheel.

Thrown from my car as it left the road,
I was later found in a ditch by some stray cows.
I could not understand what the fox
was so earnestly trying to tell me.
Why were those men burying the cemetery gates?
I became convinced that the church was melting
and I collided with a stationary truck
that was coming the other way.

Polio Ward

In '52 outside the ward with the glass roof,
summer had beaten down all visiting day.
Parents and uncles came and went away
leaving me *Coral Island*, its cover of white strands,
tumbling sea and purple mountains.
Thompson in the bed next to mine,
with his *Roy of the Rovers* and Football Annuals,
liked spitting and just before lights out,
as staff nurse left the ward for the telephone,
hit my book cover with a real gobby one.

We flailed, fell from our beds, thrashed about –
I felt no pain in my plastered leg
or he in his as I punched and kicked
and he punched and kicked.
The others laughed at first but then it changed.
Their wild cheering gained an edge
as they poled and pushed their beds
into a circle: Bates, Jenkins, Clegg
and the others – they even made a space
so Carter in the iron lung, could see.

To me their shouts seemed remote
as if miles away from the fierce urgency
of our struggle on the parquet floor.
The cheering brought Staff nurse through the door
and we were firmly dragged apart
and in a side office Doctor Parker made us shake hands.
We solemnly did. He took it in good heart
and only cuffed our hair saying if we did it again
we'd be sent off to a private room.
Going back we were heroes: Thompson's eye swelling,

blood on my pyjamas. So we got claps on the back,
even a hug from callipered Bates, who always got excited,
Jenkins and Cleggie punching the air and Carter,
snot streaming from his nose (which he couldn't wipe –
he was quadra-paralysed), his whisper barely heard,
said: *You were great, that was really great!*
and his eyes were shining with every word.

At the Edward Thomas Fellowship
Spring Walk and Dinner

That couple who lived six months of the year in Thame then six in Melbourne:
I liked the way a puzzled breeze blew across her face when I asked
their reaction to the oddness of Winter then Spring then Winter again.

Spring's not the same down under she murmured after a blank pause
as if answering a question asked by someone sitting to my right
and making a definite decision to have plain not cappuccino coffee.

Would the earth wobble on its axis if everyone by unilateral convention
followed their example in great migrations on Ladyday and Michaelmas?
Have they doppel-gängers who live in perpetual Summer and Autumn?

All the fellowship walked the Eastbury ridge that morning;
last year's nettle stalks neat paintbrush slashes against the hedges
and at the end the rushing winterbourne between village cottages.

Her husband was deaf and was maybe in yet another season:
he looked at me pointedly and asked *What flavours are there?*
and when I replied *Of what?* responded *No, I mean what flavours?*

So daffs follow celandines, campions twinkle and just as orchids spire,
celandines break the ground again and then it's daffs, campion, orchid
and a cold wind comes and you're not sure where it's from.

Concerning Monique in Burnt Oak

Dear Sir, It needs to be reported
and I think urgently
that I and my family
are in a state of crisis
since the unfortunate situation arose.

We have left our abode,
quietly as requested but under
the most strong protestation;
the circumstance was unforeseen,
our preparations were incomplete.

Now we do not have a way to turn.

For Monique (my daughter),
she is most dear to me,
her most treasured things
are the small doll's house,
and the pearly box with her first teeth,

To these we have no access.

Also she is sick to think
of the rabbits hopping about uncared for.
You must understand that she
has not been accustomed to this.
She wants her bed in her room.

We are locked away from it.

Monique (my daughter)
craves to be permitted or allowed
to hear her music and not the stuff
we always get on the TV
in our present, unwelcome, abode.

We beg permission that she gather her cassettes.

In two hours notice time simply was unavailable,
her rabbit pets were abandoned and forlorn,
all her reading materials were left -
so important to lay foundation
for accomplishment in this world.

We beg we be granted more time
in view of these extenuating circumstances
and at least time to collect the small house.
I implore you to enable us brief access.

Monique's written affidavit: 'My two rabbits
were born to be free!'

The Peewits

In this particular M4 snarl-up I endeavour
not to be stressed, typical and middle management.
I'd slowed hoping the clog was still moving;
but no. Now in front the logos smile their usual ironies:
Triumph, Acclaim, Range and Rover.

In a field beside us lapwings dive then curve up
and dive again: spring crazy, and giddy with lust.
The audio book on the machine has a hard-nosed,
female detective say *I'm outta here*
She says it twice. The thriller ends.

I read and re-read the morning agenda,
Then assemble the cassettes alphabetically.
The flat cap in the Metro picks a fight
with a white van – probably territorial.
The three lunky lads in the cabin above him

have folded expressionless arms and open Suns.
The horizon shimmers above our linear city and ahead
a plume of black smoke rises like in a war documentary.
In the nearby Nova a woman very slowly paints her nails.
The lapwings dive; share with us their sharp and sudden song.

After a Call from the Witnesses

Nothing is permanent. When they called
I'd left a laden bag on the kitchen table edge.
It slowly re-arranged its loads and balances
and, before they departed, slumped to the floor.

Another time it might have found a stasis
and so reposed indefinitely.
Not, of course, forever – nothing is permanent,
though, they assured me, their angels are.

On the Watchtower's cover they stand,
wings at rest, silver hair neatly combed –
an anxious multitude on eiderdown clouds,
fresh as if from a rapturous, body-lotioned shower.

In laundered dressing gowns surveying
the blue and cloudy planet turning below,
they seem worried, troubled. The fragrance
from their trimmed beards will last for all eternity.

Duende in Northwood Hills

This corner with the mauve lilac going over,
the dried out shiplap with one panel loose,
the little wind-vane man turning the wheel of weather
and the composite stones receiving the shed petals of a tea rose:
has this corner felt the giddy rush of the duende?

That shop in the neighbourhood parade;
the one between the freshly opened vintners
(Special Offer of Riojas to *Get the taste of Spain*)
and the tatty, closed down one that sold computers:
has it felt the coursing blood of duende through its veins?

The clay hillock behind the school called 'The Roughs'
with its hawthorn clumps, bramble tangles,
discarded porn, dog turds, frothing willowherb,
evening sodium spangle and daily drone of local cars:
has the moving spectre of the duende crossed its shadows?

And this woman beside the medical centre
with her shell suit, her neat trainers with the snub toe,
her bundled child, mad-eyed in the push chair:
as her cigarette smokes, has she felt the duende
move through her being like a river of death?

Komödie, Tate Modern

One eye sees, the other feels.   Paul Klee.

Whatever else
this team has not been concerned with analysing rainbows.
One member was once but simply could not recall her findings
and another might have contributed but was distracted by various animals.

This lack of concern proved distressing to their incumbents;
drear people who expected more commitment to research
and gave vent to their feelings in a number of buzzy musterings
in which they clad themselves aggressively in reds and turquoise.

But in the end nothing was published – no honours with-held,
no medals on banded ribbon ripped from bodice or dirndl.

All along the team's conversations explored a different table of elements
and during these discourses they were soothed by the soft boom
of Tibetan gongs. Not many things could be universally accepted
but those benign vibrations were.

It was all in a spindrift season
with papery flowers and bulging schools of fungi.

In the end the rush of spores tainted everything.
Gears crashed, structures developed cracks
and the floor was showered with discarded logarithms.

Scarcely noticed though – cast from the beveled edge
of nearby oriel windows, were tiny prisms
banding, as they had to, the glancing sun's
eternal sample range of colours.

To Capture Endymion

That bluebell –
I would have one like it,
exactly like it, to the filigree detail
but in purest glass.

Glass thin as the thinnest petal wall,
imbued with dyes
steeped deep in complicated blueness
containing mauves, pinks and greys
and tipped with the white/yellow powdery splay
of minute teeth each ending a wisp of unseen silica.

And the stem – pure in its thrust,
its liquid, tubular shaft dusted with the finest dust,
the whole moving through a sombre spectrum
of deep greens, to brown, to blue,
the crook angled precise to the millionth.

And within this glass,
buried scents, essences
of awakening woodland
tinged with garlics, semen and honey.

Each morning a first act –
spraying mist on the delicate surfaces,
their curves, pendants and silences.
The water in shining domes
on flat green blades of unblemished basal leaves
fresh as the day before the last bud opened.

Each morning the same – eternal, unchanging,
the glass strong as strongest metals,
colours constant as light broken through a prism.

And that splay of opening beech leaves –
make it glass
and the tree,
the whole intricate thicket,
make glass –

the whole breathing wood,
make glass.

Sorting Old Kodachromes

Ones I didn't take
like something said
by someone else

but in my language
and offering an intimacy
that was not invited.

My own a flood
of intricate detail:
softness of light

on a Saxon wall,
snowdrops just over
at the foot of a gravestone,

contact almost tangible.
In others: people,
heads full of the fleet moment,

smiling at the lens,
defying the future,
writhing trees behind them.

Colours drain,
dust specks mar
a bright mouth.

And this woodland edge
with April flecks of green,
the branches still

as if the wind
was arrested,
the planet stopped turning.

Only the frozen clouds
seem mutable -
as if they were today's clouds somehow.

After Matthew's Gap

It was in a Merc somewhere outside Bangkok –
the driver wanted to overtake this van,
'He's carrying durian', he said. 'What's that?' I asked,

then it came through the a/c, a stench you wouldn't believe.
They're banned in hotels but taste of sweet custard.
They look like grenades. They auction them as aphrodisiacs

There was a scorpion the size of a tea-plate
on a path north of Chiang Mai. They have the same word there
for hello, goodbye and thank you. Matthew paused.

Grandfather said that in the desert he'd lost his asthma,
It was the air of course. This reminded Matthew's mother
of the army transports buried in the sandstorm

she'd seen in 'The English Patient' the night before.
She added that Gillian and Donald were going to Guatemala,
The Yucatan peninsula she added helpfully.

Matthew chased a piece of meat around his plate.
The only lake in Sumatra is in an extinct volcano –
one of its islands is the same size as Singapore.

The Sultan of Brunei can fit the entire population of the country
in his reception hall. There are people in the jungle there
who still worship animals, we didn't see them though.

Isabelle craved durians when she was pregnant,
said his mother, *her husband got her two in Paris, vacuum wrapped.*
I never slept anywhere as well as in the desert. said Grandfather.

The fut-futs by the hostel say the Reclining Buddha's closed
even when it isn't - they're paid to take you to 'Gem-store! Gem Store!'
They never close. Grandfather said it was like that in Jerusalem.

KL was OK. We didn't go up the two towers, only the radio mast.
In the square they say they have the highest flag pole in Asia.
I told them I'd spoken to Gillian and Donald before they left:

they liked travelling near war zones and staying in B & B's
because all the Hiltons and Marriotts look the same, anyway
Donald enjoys a bit of edge. Cambodia last year was hairy though.

Here it's been the wettest autumn in 60 years said Grandfather
and that got us onto monsoons, El Niño and mega-tsunamis.
Matthew fell asleep. *Poor thing,* said his mother, *him and his jet lag.*

When They are Both Full Grown

It was in full swing with the yule log blazing,
the smell of roasting chestnuts,
Camilla being daft under the mistletoe
and Auntie Grace in spout about how many
berries she has on her ornamental holly.
A blur of people in our country kitchen
were opening and shutting the new units
with their crafty placement of death-watch
flight holes that look absolutely authentic –
Marisa's little man did them with a tiny drill.
I was pouring a grapey Chardonnay
for the new people from 'Woodland Edge',
was in mid sentence with a story
about the hedge-laying we'd had done at the front
when Kate materialized and was tugging my arm:
What is it? I said through a clenched smile.
You must come she replied simply.
With a wave at the Simpsons who were admiring
that imitation Grinling Gibbons ivy in the hall,
I followed her to the conservatory.
Look she said.

Outside the trees were shrinking.
The beeches, the cherries, the Japanese maple
the Turkey oak, the balsam poplar;
shrinking with sighs as quiet as snow falling.
Shrinking into themselves,
the Arborvitae, the mountain ash –
becoming low, ground hugging,
like those ancient northern birches
that live through three month nights
under ice storms and pitiless blizzards,
flattening themselves into crevices and lees
never more than inches off the freezing wastes
of Iceland, Novaya Zemlya and the Arctic tundra.

Geese in a Market Crowd

Not a quack, gabble or mutter
as the six thread through chaos.

The mountains seem to be liquefying
this damp and blustered morning,

the sky is hesitant and lacks confidence –
so the geese are a certainty in what is shapeless.

They waddle, chittering in concentration –
their foolish feet, their pert rears

an order in the hopeless tumble
of junk mathematics around them.

I Think Continually

Barnes Att. bijou actress's 3rd floor hideaway.
View of boat race for 3/4 sec. (Roy Brooks Advert 1960s)

On Finals day in 1961
across a corner of shaved grass
and just before the men's doubles
I saw Monty. He was listening
to a pretty girl in an apricot dress;
I heard him say *'Well, actually...'*

I was at the Building Exhibition in '64
examining the stand promoting
cavity trays and wall ties.
Alec Douglas-Home and three anxious
men in suits that seemed too tight
approached me. *'Quite right, quite right'* he said.

On the twelfth at Moor Park
after the housebuilder's boozy lunch
in the hospitality tent
I was looking at the silver birches
when Gerald Ford strode past
saying *'Here take this'* to his caddy.

Just by the Bird of Paradise plants
in the Palm garden at Reids
I was reading a brochure about
bargain Christmas breaks when
Lord Carrington on a balcony above
said *'I think so, don't you'* to his wife.

Climbing over the stile at Chequers
I took the path beside Hampden wood
and watched Denis Thatcher
hit drive after drive towards
the South Africa monument.
I could just hear the snick of club on ball.

And I was in Whitehall
that sunny day in May.
Every one seemed happy, smiley
and simple. I shook the hand
of the new Prime Minister;
'Yes. Yes..' he said.

Battlefield +(+)

Preparing to enjoin, they do not see the clapboard,
the stacked blocks and timbers in the builder's yard
nor the dual-carriageway. Banners riffle in a slight breeze.

The infantry calmly take up their planned positions
as two anglers cycle by, one leaning back with hands
off the handlebars. It is late morning.

Archers form rank half in and half out a retail warehouse;
snorting cavalry shuffle amidst the screams of children
playing on the park swings. The tension is palpable.

An ice-cream van trills around the nearby estate.
The first cries across the car-park are ignored
by the shell-suit woman loading her boot.

The thunder of hooves and bellowed huzzahs
do not concern the kid clattering his skate-board
down the concrete ramp; nor the deadly waves of arrows.

Following ranks leap groaning bodies of the first
wielding axe and shield at massed formations
beside the filling station with its plastic flags.

The engagement is thickest where the speed bumps
put in last year, successfully calm the traffic.
There is terrible slaughter in the chemist's extended

cosmetics department. The new assistant frowns
as she works out how to use the electric cash register
and a spearman, head pumping blood, slumps across

the toiletries counter. A woman asks for cotton balls.
At the head of the bus queue two knights clang swords
hand to hand. A schoolgirl blows a pink bubble

as the single-decker drones in past their foaming horses.
The conflict ebbs and flows through the overcast afternoon.
When the corner estate agent brings in his 'A' boards,

auxiliaries arrive across a field of rape. They clinch it.
There is a messy withdrawal down the back gardens
of 'Willow Ridge Crescent' and 'The Maltings'.

Panic sets in as the first home-bound executives turn
from the motorway. It ends in a rout by the sewage farm.
Cattle move towards a gate. The sodiums come on.

Victory cheers are unnoticed by plumed youths
gooning and looning around the corpses
strewn by the vandalized memorial fountain.

At Harefield Manor ✝

Notice first the half buried brick arches.
They'd held beehives for self-made Sir Thomas —
honey to sweeten hams, sugared viands
for a cantankerous, balding, black toothed Queen.
We park under the sycamores.

She'd listened to eulogies of welcome
beneath a massive elm
from players dressed as *Time* and *Place*.
It rained in torrents so she remained in saddle,
her face expressionless and very still.

Harefield mud is thick,
its grasping clay clings to our boots.
The Manor's garden walls are crumbling;
they lead to the vacant eyes of old East Lodge.
Suburban houses crawl over the near hill.

From behind the coppiced hazel,
a gypsy leads a black horse, an ancient mare,
by clutching the hair between her ears.
She descends the sucking path to a low stable
in a fuzz of flies, her spavined legs stumbling.

He says *She's thirty now.*
Don't like being out midday.
Them dirt flies lay eggs. She prefers shade.
She stands motionless in the shadows,
not watching as he forks hay into her manger.

On the 31st July 1602, Elizabeth I was guest of Sir Thomas Egerton at his Mansion House in Harefield. There were four days of pageantry and feasting but it poured with rain throughout her stay. The old house burned down in 1669 but the Lodge and traces of the garden walls remain.

Conspiracies

The 'phone call was not overheard.
The reported car wasn't there,
the roadside empty, just cabbage whites floating.

Low roof, dribbling fountain, dog-less kennel
and inside men in grey murmur in a windowless room.
They are miles from the buttercups.

Each page of that issue, a casket of secrets.
Two wait beside fruit machines, no flight plan logged;
only pigeons are airborne over the orchard.

Much talk of snakes but none seen locally
and the address in Toulouse proved to be false.
Schoolgirls bask on a grassy knoll.

The deceased was sighted in Rio, a witness confirmed
but the bulletin posted later was inconsequential.
The woman in the estanco was known by no-one.

The Los Angeles kitchen was a crypt of knives and eyes.
A gathering took place in a bone dry wadi,
but later accounts made no reference to local fauna.

The tunnel in Paris proved inviolable concrete.
An hour later there was but one aircraft aloft
amongst the assassin clouds and high swallows.

Watched for hours. No-one left, no-one came.
Then, on the webcam, a lone figure passed between doors
a long way from the whispering beeches.

It is said

The snowdrops had opened in the Lammas woods
when the Abbott and his two companions
greeted the lone horseman approaching the Postern Gate.
Was the message to bring hope or early despair?

Entowered alone the Gentle Lady dreamed of her dead son,
her eyes misting at the sword gash in the carved escutcheon.
Faithful John had spied ravens south on the chapel spire.
This omen fretted the brows of the young lords murmuring

by the wide hearth lined with crests of attainted estates.
Word came that the old oak had fallen so cottars
were ordered to dig a deep moat. The proud daughter
gazed with passive fixity to the east her ring untarnished.

It had been a winter of storms and whirling snow.
In the north tower the Old Duke's quill scratched urgently
but the Great Hall was silent save for the scuttle of mice.
A single horn pierced the silent air of early dusk.

News from France! The coachman hurried across the yard
and an ancient key was turned in the refectory lock.
It is said that that night a wing fell from a ceiling putto
and dashed the Knight's wine from his lifted cup.

Banners, quartered with Griffin Couchant,
lowered as crested knights set boldly north
whilst in the Chapel the Great Lord slept, feet on a hedgehog,
his lady beside him, her nose knocked off.

In three months daffodils flecked the demesne coppice
as a chill wind blew warnings through the spring Marches.
She held the babe high to the west mullions
and then ....

The Russians at the Garden Centre

Her large feet encased in spiked heels
    the colour of glacé cherry. Her legs long –
        their anatomy clear, each muscle honed,

each tendon flexed.
    Her waist insect narrow,
        a breath of skirt across the top of tough thighs.

Her fall of hair is asphalt black –
    her mouth a slash of magenta on chalk white.
        Charcoal dust lines her eyes.

She is a foot and a half taller than her tubby escort
    with his Khruschev dome, mirrored shades
        and energetic waddle.

Behind, the landscape is blocked by their minder –
    a rectangle of grey, topped by a broad neck,
        a chipped and lipless mouth.

His wrists seem as thick as his neck.
    They pause by a stand of succulents.
        A tall *Cereus nobilis* is erect,

spined and squirting a spermy white flower at its tip.
    She leans forward with interest.
        Cactus she says.

Clearing the Notebook

'Your poetry is too much about things'   Publisher's comment

– As I approached the motorway
the Red Devil jets were around me like roaring swifts,
in the windscreen, the mirrors, above and to the side,
then sudden over roofs, then a streak through trees.

– We crested the hill and found the valley beeches
white and glassy with frost and on a stagged oak,
three Red Kites. One launched and with steady wings
beat across the coin of sun that gleamed behind mist.

– Outside Deya the evening lengthened shade
in the motionless olive grove above the sea.
A nightingale sang three yards away
and on a stone a Painted Lady spread its wings.

– Dawn stop near Murcia at a quarry town,
and in the blue gloom noticing everything was pale,
coated with dust: trees, house-windows and men
inside the bar who were shouting and sinking cogñacs.

– That other dawn place in Somiedo,
the projecting shelf just below the ridge,
counting thirty Egyptian vultures one by one
as they dropped to catch the plain's first thermals.

– That time we made love in the bluebell wood,
the scent of young flowers, a gentle breeze,
the dog snuffling over in the rabbit warren –
it was years ago and it was a poem.

After the Thirteen

— After the king was mated,
further moves were made
amid the involved labyrinths
of black's queen side fianchetto.
Chinking blackbirds
on the shadowy terraces of A5
witnessed the futile argument
of these unresolved concerns.

— In the tree
that seemed to contain three blackbirds,
there were four blackbirds.
The fourth,
concealed behind the trunk,
was unaware of the role
it had missed in American Literature.

— A blackbird flitted
from the fence top
to the cherry bough,
from the cherry bough
to the lawn edge
thence back
to the cherry bough
and from there
to the fence top.
Many have commented
on the pointlessness
of these movements.

— Because Wild Carrot
has a single purple flower
centring a whorl
of one hundred white flowers,
I think I understand the jar in Tennessee.
All would return to being mysterious
if upon the jar
there perched a blackbird.

— A car was parked
in July shade.

On the steering wheel
a blackbird

waiting.

A Bit of Gertrude Stein Inaccurately Remembered

Vide the sea eagle.
            He dives on a flock of starlings.
    His only chance
is to select one, just one –
        not the plumpest, or tastiest looking,
                the stupidest or apparently slowest –
        no just one.
a singleton in the many –
        that's how its done:
                obsessed, acid-etched focus.

    But then exactitude is exactly exactitude
and shutters shut and shutters shut –
        for Napoleon is Napoleon
                and the sea crashes under quite indifferent;
        crashes, fills and drains,
offering now and then a green wall of glass,
        and behind it shoals of silver tunny.
                History teaches
    a sudden glimpse may be allowed –
    but I've not experienced it
            exactly exactly.

Encounter

Two approach in blue shirts.
These are the two I have been expecting.
I calculate: soft/hard maybe hot/cold
or green/red even black/white. The bar is very long
and sinuous, moving into shadows
like the end of a tunnel made out of mirrors
facing one another. The two become mid-ground
then suddenly fore-ground with all the detail.

An envelope is searched for and found.
The carpet has a hole; the surviving sisal threads
make a grid like a city seen from the air.
One speaks. The other riffles paper and sits,
his blue shirt still showing the fold marks
from the display state when he bought it.
Maybe there are still some pins in the folds.
I hear the wind outside.

They seem to me not wholly urban,
not wholly suburban. Whatever they are,
they are not rustic. Somewhere in the mix though
medium density housing with precise parking ratios.
Outside the buildings are ghosts along the artery.
The sky slants to the left.
We are in a place outside the book.
One writes but his pen is transparent
and absolutely silent.

Jin Mao

Lola said she'd cried when the lift opened
onto the golden light of the atrium:
'It was like nothing I'd ever seen before.

We'd only gone for a coffee with Carrie's friend
and in the lift you don't feel you're going up
and then wham! That golden aura. It's indescribable.

Later that day I went to the park near Carrie's,
I needed to be on my own for a bit but I left
by a different gate to the one I'd gone in –

they all look the same until you're outside.
Everything looked so weird and strange, I panicked.
Then I remembered the teahouse rendezvous

so I went to a traffic cop and made tea drinking signs
and he pointed just as I heard my grand daughter's shout
and Carrie waving from the opposite pavement.

That afternoon we saw some jade Buddhas;
not the usual fat, overstuffed ones but young
and handsome Buddhas. And the jade was white.

I didn't know you could get white jade.
They were so serene not like the twisted pain,
blood and thorns we have to put up with

but a sort of radiance like in that wonderful atrium.'
She couldn't remember who designed the Jin Mao but said
it was the third highest in the world and had sixty lifts.

Alicante: The Beggar   +

At Manolin we ate fat prawns
with Remedios, Mari and Merced;
fat prawns and a velvety Rioja
that made our words rich,
comfortable and at ease.

They drove us back to 'Le Palas'
and declined a nightcap
but as we left the car
we were suddenly with
and of a beggar.

He became entwined with us;
his persistence clinging
and enfolded in somehow
so that he seemed within the car
as well as out.

And so much was he
between and beside us, he became
with us on our drive from Manolin,
sitting there, a smell,
then walking with us

from the door and leaving
with us from the table,
fast tight and lodged
in our comfortable words;
hooked tight to our laughter.

He then pursued us into the laze
of the day before and into
the plane the day before that;
he spread, a stain, into before that
and before that

until he had always been there;
his whining monotone,
tugging our sleeves,
sinking his nails, sinking nails
into our soft flesh.

Now and Now Again

Crikey! she said
    as the two seater rounded the chicane –
there was the blue Levantine ocean – blue as a poster,

one white scratch of a speedboat,
    a frilly bottom to impossible cliffs,
the coast spreading on and on.

What chimed?
    The sudden wild nowness of it.

And that time Tony headed his journal's opening page
    'A Grecian Odyssey' just before
we dumped the snagged anchor at Spetsai.

It was as far as he got.
    He wanted his quest recorded for a future grandchild
but the now and now and now again drowned it.

Donaghy claimed that 'now' was three seconds long –
    one to see, one to imbibe and one to remember.
The fourth second started another three.

She went faster on the straight.

Unnervingly fast. Zip-zip the other way
    then a final zip much less than a three second now
and that's all that is recorded.

*'Furthermore, they say, the brain possesses an auditory information
'buffer' of three seconds worth of information (There! Now you know
how long the present is!)'*
    Michael Donaghy 'Wallflowers: 'Reading in Rhythm' p23

After the Uffizi

At Bar Vecchio the girl in the corner
is unaware of the wild roses
that stream from her mouth.

Her companion shouldering a bow
shaped like his upper lip conceals
hocks and hooves beneath the table.

Soon he'll clop across the cobbles
past four nuns with huge pigeon wings
and tiny hands in reverent prayer.

They will ignore an abandoned baby lying in straw
beside a motorbike revved by a youth with red cap,
bum-freezer cloak and painted-on hose.

The old boy dozing at the bar
has forgotten the disc of his halo.
Above him, obese and tumbling cupids.

Ascension of Isola San Giulio

In the late afternoon the island loosened moorings
and drifted towards the town. The approach was silent
and hardly noticed until waters became turbulent

and the quays met in a long grinding kiss.
Boardwalks splintered and cracked but not before
the brides and their entourages had disembarked.

The convent doors stayed closed.
This service rendered, the island moved slowly back
as clouds mottled sunlight on the lakeside mountains.

All was calm. Townspeople gathered open mouthed
and heard from over the water, on a gentle breeze,
choiring voices from the nuns. A sweet imploring chant

as with scarce a shudder the island began to rise.
There was a basal rending of rock, the campanili tolled
and with unwavering force San Giulio lifted free of the lake,

water streaming from the rising banks
where motor boats dangled like tiny pendants until one by one
their painters broke and they fell with other debris.

The lake erupted with splashes like a white blossom
as the island moved steadily towards the sky
its shadow crossing San Mauricio and Santuario del Sasso.

When it entered the first wisps of cumulus,
the stacked clouds above opened outspread arms
and the island was engulfed. All became a swirl of vapour.

The onlookers stared upwards and at the now visible far shore.
There were a few remnant splatters in the vacant water
then just bird song above and around the weeping brides.

The convent island of San Giulo near the lakeside town of Orta in Northern
Italy is a favourite site for wedding photographs.

Of the Night

Leaving Calle Perpetua Socorro,
we nudge the car into the shuffling
outbound lane. It's rush hour. Winter.

We reach the city edge,
passing neoned cheap hotels,
and hoardings with enormous grins.

It's here we first catch sight
of their pale white legs,
white stilettos, slashes of lipstick -

the teenage hookers.
They line a zone of sodium shadows
and as we pass we catch only glimpses.

On a closed service station forecourt
one waggles her backside to the traffic
as she puffs a slim cigarette.

Another flashes budding breasts
and her coltish companion feigns a laugh
as if they were at a crowded party.

We take the blacktop into the mountains.
Our head-lights pick out rabbits.
They stare and stare then bolt,

scut bobbing
as they make for pine scrub
and the sheltering dark.

The Flowering

Our air is filled with malignant pollen.
All our havens are queasy with doubt.

Beneath calm lime boughs,
in a boulevard of prams and tricycles,

the dust-caked lorry
will explode.

Soft blossom will incinerate
and curl.

Amongst children with silly hats,
trilling on a dappled concourse,

a youth will become one
with spinning glass

and rising stamens of blood.
There will be no silence like the following silence.

The doors, ceilings and living rooms
that contain our house

of films and paper, rugs and tile,
petal-like, will rush apart.

All that we are to become billowing dust.
Our fences will crack and blaze.

The Last Week

i.m. Michael Donaghy

Ruairi's pawn chain was mad
and your rooks locked weirdly in the centre.
Next morning, the pieces shattered,
just the chess clock ticking.

Voices floated up from the orchard,
Ruairi's piping, your low murmur.
Later some almonds and green lemons
abandoned on the outside shelf.

Drifting stall to stall at the rastro,
you touched my arm, *Hey look at this*:
a plaster cast of a white, exhausted face.
Some guy's death mask you whispered.

And after you left I checked the player.
Your CD of recordings was still inside –
the first track, three minutes of bird song,
the second, half an hour of thunder and rain.

*Michael Donaghy tutored a writing course at Almassera Vella in
September 2004. He was accompanied by his wife Maddy and son
Ruauri. He died in London less than a week after the course concluded.*

Late Chain Survey

We dragged the chain towards the vague margin,
    the field for us the only field on earth,

all else was blur. We'd formed the sight line,
    behind us upright rods of red and white

and the one set distant in front. Twilight fell.
    Beyond the boundary hedges all faded to black.

Our thin tape rasped out offsets and ties
    the rye grass offering no mark,

the same in one station as the next.
    Then you took the chain forward,

your figure questing on into dark -
    then link and link, there was only the moving chain.

Taino +

He knew the ridge above Pico de Pedrera.
Each morning he saw the sun catch its flank –
that instant, just as the roosters started up.

Then came the rattling of blinds,
Inmaculada flicking water to settle the dust
and a sudden cracked note from the church tower.

Coffee, tostada with oil,
his older brother fiddling with a shotgun
and grunting as he left for the truck to the mill.

That's how it had been day following day,
so he was surprised at the force of his brother's embrace
and his gruff kiss when he left for Cordoba and the front.

His mothers face grey, her smile of stone -
he'd not seen that before either.
Cards from the poker game with his younger brothers

were still splayed on the table –
there was a centimetre left in the wine bottle.
That was 1936 in Benilloba. It's an Arab name.

*Federico Borrell Garcia, 'Taino' from Benilloba, near Alcoy was photographed
at the moment of his death in a skirmish at Cerro Muriano near Cordoba
by Robert Capa on the 5th September 1936. The photograph 'Falling
Militiaman' became one of the best known images of the Spanish Civil War.*

"They Were Just Going to Work"

Anonymous interviewee.   Madrid, March 11th 2004

Every moment is charged,
>   crammed and packed,

even that dull wall passing
>   and that exhausted building.

Fill this torpor –
>   revere the gawping posters,

smear their essence over you,
>   be of them, inside them,

let your every nerve cell
>   lap up and experience them.

Enjoy the sudden blank and thunder
>   of the tunnel black.

Draw everything from the couple crossing a road,
>   the vague man on the corner,

the child, the child's bike,
>   the child's school rucksack.

Capture the universe locked in a trackside leaf,
>   in each dust mote,

uncover the architecture of a window raindrop,
>   its dense geologies of colour.

Feed on this quotidian plenitude.
>   Clutch at everything. Drain all dry.

Rise in wonder
>   at the towers of your approaching city.

Couple

She's dumped the South African.
He was in St Lucia. *Winged keel trouble*
he'd said but she'd been sent some candids
by that Argentinean she'd met in Gstaad.

He said he wouldn't sell them, no way,
but she knew he would. It was just like
that time in Puerto Rico with the Korean girl,
all grovelling apologies and a trip to Dubai.

She wanted to shuck off the feel of it all
so flew La Guardia to Dresden.
She rang her mother's flat in Barcelona
from the private suite in the departure lounge.

Just back from Hampstead my dear,
so nice to see the twins, if just for an afternoon.
Planes climb and descend. Others scratch across the sky.
Australia is on fire, Burma engulfed in mud.

A week later his fore-sail blew: 300,000 dollars.
It was somewhere off Gomera,
well off the press pack radar
so they'd lost interest and his sponsors didn't like that.

He tried all her numbers.
I'm away. Leave a message if you have to.
He flew Gran Canaria to Goa via Rome.
Got to get away, he said, *got to do some thinking.*

The Pursuit

'Every day they grew more violent, every day they grew more nude...'
                                            Peter Cook and Dudley Moore

Near dusk the managers broke from the building
pursued by swift and furious nudes.
Above, the firmament filled with cherubim
who joined the chase, enraged and tumbling.

They crossed the financial district, its darkened towers,
then fled down a wide and littered boulevard
as from doorways and out of tunnels further nudes
joined the keening stampede.

Passing plinths with shattered statuary,
there was the slap of a thousand feet
and a rush of frantic wings in the air above
as from the porches of the battered suburb

more nude furies rushed to join the throng.
Exhausted the managers arrived in the city wastelands
and as the sun collapsed below a distant line of hills,
the nudes fell upon them, rending their garments,

tearing and ripping their flesh with bare nails
to leave them flayed and naked in the gathering night.

The Knife

All has become alabaster-still and those assembled
crave that the room's air stay motionless,
every molecule remain in stasis, every breath inaudible.
They are perched, slumped or stand frozen,
their minds locked onto this desired equilibrium.
A terminal shadow moves across the tableau
fingering detail by detail the crockery's secrets

and making silent traverse of each arrested figure.
The window nets shimmer with a whispered exhalation –
eyes flick soundlessly from eye to eye
then settle back to stare when movement ceases.
Hanging pictures depict a gaudy sunset,
a lone triumphant mountaineer on a cloudy summit,
laughing children with kites in a meadow.

A solitary fly thuds the fanlight.
Eyes flick once more. From the still trees a bird call.
There had been a long silence before it
and they wish for a long silence to follow.
Their cups are towered, plates balanced on edge.
A faint moan of wind from a distant tundra –
someone drops a knife. The universe ends.

The Day of Dust

At midday St Peter's dome collapsed upon itself.
The roar was heard along the yellow Tiber.
The Chrysler tower laid its length across the Commodore
and dust-clouds billowed up 42nd street.
Silver cladding of the Guggenheim
flapped and clattered through mute suburbs of Bilbao
and with a deep sigh Cheops sunk level with the desert.

The Eiffel tower became a chaos of twisted steel
and a groaning Campanile di San Marco fell into the lagoon.
The Tower of London vaporised, shells of Sydney's Opera House
became crushed and broken. Golden Gate swayed, cables
twanged and snapped as Rushmore's figures avalanched
onto their scree. Angkor Wat was dust – the Taj a heap of stones
and the terraces of Bath fell like dominoes.

Hagia Sophia exploded into a shroud of dust,
the golden pavilion of Kyoto slipped forward into water,
stones of Great Zimbabwe became the earth,
the Parthenon a heap of fluted drums. Thebes became dust,
Heathrow a tower of flames, Sagrada Familia a mound of rubble.
The bridge at Avignon was broken.
Fragments of Liberty covered Ellis Island.

Boulder dam was breached in a thunder of water,
stones of the Great Wall scattered over the Gobi desert
and St Edwards Tower slumped into the House of Commons.
The Pantheon fell, Stonehenge fell, the Coliseum crumpled.
The Lloyds building unravelled as if violently shaken,
the paving of Tiananmen subsided into earth
and the turrets of Ludwig's Schloss dropped into the gorge.

The fall of Chartres echoed over the grain fields of Beauce
and Madrid's four towers became a single heap.
Petra shivered into pink dust. Jerusalem's wall became dust.
The Dome of the Rock became dust. The filigree walls
of the Alhambra rumbled into the ravine,

Rio's Redeemer crashed into the city from Corcovado
and Burj Al Arab blew in fragments across the Persian Gulf.

Pampas ants joined their cities to form a highway
from the Pyrenees to the Dolomites.
Barbary apes swung in the trees of Kensington.
The cone of Kilimanjaro was bare.

Thessalonians ✝

We who are still alive and are left will be caught up together....

And then we were falling.
The air rushed in our ears
and loosened our clothes.

Beneath our feet there was nothing,
We fell towards nothing.
Beside us the Frobishers were falling.

He still held his keys
and Pattie was upside down,
one loose shoe chasing her.

The newly-weds from the corner
were falling – the gap between
their outstretched hands grew wider.

It was all in silence.
The children from the flats
were falling like tossed dolls -

one clutched a cell phone
in her fat little hand.
Other youths were falling.

They thrashed about them
trying to catch the air.
Clouds gathered around,

swirling clouds of falling people.
Their dense multitudes darkened the sky.
Then the silence ceased.

Temple

I would construct a temple of silence
with whatever idle stone
has fallen from the mountain.

Air would play through its columns.
One frieze would depict folly,
another the hard shape of dreams.

Within there would be frescos
of mustering birds in a tree
and a single idealised cornflower.

There would be steps,
each of a different hardwood,
ascending them like moving up into song.

The temple would crown a gentle hill
forested with sweet chestnut and beech,
ghost orchids rising from the leaf mould.

Over the years wind would smooth away folly,
would erase the shape of dreams
but not the single cornflower.

The mustered birds would scatter.

The Tree

The tree in the stairwell made our light penumbral,
brown – like a Dovedale stream
or sunlight through thick Victorian glass.

The spreading boughs formed another ceiling
hiding away our ornate roses,
our plaster cornices. It was a ceiling of swishing leaves.

Moving through the spaces of our house
we liked placing a hand on the warm bark.
We rolled up all our Persian rugs
so we could walk on timber with bare feet.

Before sleep we touched foreheads to the living trunk
and on waking listened to the tree's morning murmurs.

It became the green heart of our house,
part of our fulsome library, our cool drawing-room.
It was a benign and growing canopy.

Three on the Scarp ✝

For Rod and Jem

It was enjoyable, the three of us
walking over the hill from Cockshoot Wood;
enjoyable because it was a day when
the round certainty of the planet
with its parent sun and daughter moon
became part of the experience. Jem said
that the three weeks of October rain
had washed out impurities leaving
the air clear as soaked glass
and so it seemed. Enjoyable the
line of the field margins,
the clumping of the woodland
and the horizon divide
                    between earth and sky.

So we walked over it, sensing the three
weeks of rain in the sodden earth,
the villages of fungus in the boles
of green and black, the draggled
flowers of late campions and the clarity
of shadows.
        With three:
one could propose an action,
one could oppose
and the third deliberate.
It was simple:
the earth the sky
and that which is there to witness them,
feel assured by them, be between them.
There is the topside of a leaf and
the underside of a leaf and, of course,
the leaf itself.

That day trinities were everywhere.

Other books published by Oversteps